Daily Oats

Sam Ed Spence

Cover: Horses In Farmland by John F. Herring, Jr.

Edited by John Records

Layout by Ken Fraser

P.O. Box 91640
Los Angeles, CA 90009
(310) 419-1640
www.racetrackchaplaincy.org

Daily Oats

Printed in the United States of America
Health Communications, Inc.
Deerfield Beach, FL

Race Track Chaplaincy of America
P.O. Box 91640
Los Angeles, CA 90009

Art Credits

Special thanks and sincere appreciation to the following artists and/or art owners who have allowed us to reproduce their work in this volume.

Tom Chapman, Redwood City, CA, www. Chapman-arts. com; tchapman@jps.net. *A Clean Break* (Day l); *Who'll Go to the Lead* (Day 9); *Disturbingthepeace* (Day 11); *Seabiscuit* (Day 21); *Getting the Kinks Out* (Day 29).

Russell Houston, Edgar, AZ, Houston Designs, 800/776-1594, www.russellhouston.com. *At the River's Edge* (Day 3).

Chuck DeHaan, Graford, TX, Chuck DeHaan Studios, 940/664-2111. *Kentucky Blue* (Day 5); *Mustangers* (Day 10); *Stage to Deadwood* (Day 15); *Kentucky Gray* (Day 22); *Spooked* (Day 25); *Up the Chisholm* (Day 31).

Jodie Boren, Abilene, TX. *Like Father - Like Son* (Day 7).

Jack Sorenson, Amarillo, TX, Rich Wiseman, LLC, 505/466-1927. *Counting His Blessings* (Day 17); *Greased Lightnin'* (Day 19).

Fred Fellows, Sonoita, AZ, 520/455-5010. *Where Two or More Are Gathered* (Day 13).

Kay Griffith, Salado, TX, 254/947-3177, griffithart@earthlink. net., *Daily Oats* (Day 18).

June Dudley, College Station, TX, 979/776-7222; Toh-Atin Gallery & Publishing Co., 800/509-3888. *An Apple a Day* (Day 23).

Gail Steiger, Prescott, AZ, owner of the **George Phippen** painting, *Tying the Knots in the Devil's Tail* (Day 27).

Dedication

This book is dedicated to our four children: Tonya Spence, our teaching evangelist-dream catcher; Tammy Hitchcock, whose gifted hands on the reins are matched only by her supple hands as a mother of five (now eight); Dondi Kingsbury, our multi-talented, globe-traveling exhorter; and David Spence, our surfing, science teacher-preacher...all blessings from the Lord that make our lives a delight.

Introduction

As horses being put through their paces need their daily grain rations, so do Christians need their daily helpings of God's Word to successfully run the race of life. This little volume is designed to give you a leg-up on understanding and meditating the Word. Use it in the morning to help jump-start your day, or as you turn in for a good night's rest.

Daily Oats is not about religion; it's about relationship... an *intimate* relationship between you—a believer—and the Creator of the universe.

The relationship began the moment you accepted Jesus Christ as your personal Savior. It will continue throughout eternity because of what Jesus accomplished for you through His time on this earth, culminated by His death, burial, and resurrection.

These thirty-one devotions, one for each day of the month, are written to help you receive what Jesus has made available as you run the race. We encourage you to look up the Bible verses included at the end of the devotion. The Holy Spirit will show you something different each time you read the devotion, especially as you search out the scriptures.

Always keep in mind...God is totally on your side, His love is unconditional, His mercy is endless, and He yearns to be your very best friend. *Oh, taste and see that the Lord is good;* (Psalm 34:8). *His* oats are delicious!

A special thanks to Chaplain Pete Crisswell and Reverend Ed Donnally, a couple of vintage jockeys, for joining me in producing these devotions. Also, a special appreciation to retired chaplain Homer Tricules, who published the first Daily Oats for his New Jersey race trackers in the 1970's.

Chaplain Sam Ed Spence

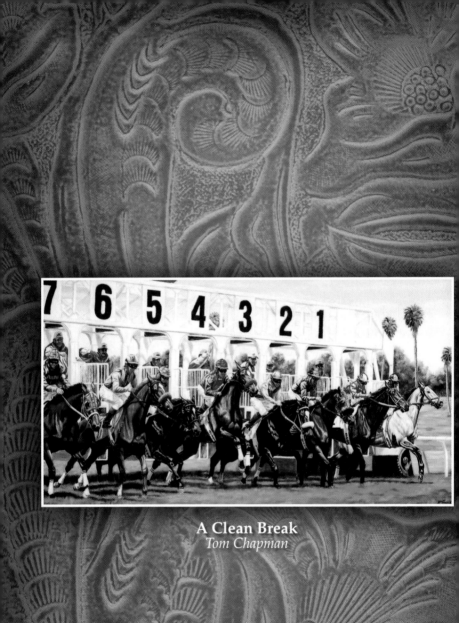

A Clean Break
Tom Chapman

A Clean Start

*So let's walk right up to him and get what he is so
ready to give. Take the mercy, accept the help.*
Hebrews 4:16 The Message

Some of the most important folks at a race track are
the starter and his assistants—the gate crew. It's
their job to see that each horse in the race gets a fair
and equal chance out of the gate. The starter wants every horse to have all four feet on the ground before he
mashes that little button that blasts the gate open.

Regardless of any horse's track record, the starter
wants every individual to have a clean break from the
gate. That's the same way Jesus is about you and me
in this *race of life*. In fact, He *gave* His life and actually
became our sin so that we could have a clean start. The
moment we accepted Jesus as our Savior, He totally
eradicated all the sin from our chart book—then led us
into the starting gate and made sure we were standing
on all fours, with the best opportunity possible to make
it to the winner's circle.

Probably no horse is really aware of all the painstaking
care the starter and his crew take in making sure the
runners get a clean start. Likewise, few Christians realize the price God paid for our fresh, clean starts. However, unlike the gate crew (whose job is basically over

once the horses leave the gate), Jesus (in the person of the Holy Spirit) stays with us all the way to the finish line.

Whenever we make a bobble, He's there to pick us up... to encourage us...to be the strength in the midst of our weakness. Again, too few of us realize He is so available, so willing, so forgiving, so desiring to be our help in the time of need. Too often our pride, guilt, or feelings of unworthiness rob us from running directly to Him, confessing our shortcoming and getting our need met.

Jesus wants us to know that regardless of how we performed on our last out, we can walk into the gate with our head held high, ready to go again. I can hear Him saying, "Come on, son, because of the blood I shed, you're getting a clean start...let's go win this one."
Sam Ed Spence

1 Timothy 2:6   *Hebrews 4:16*
2 Corinthians 5:21   *Romans 8:31-32*

He gave His life and
actually became our sin so
that we could have
a clean start.

Jesus Loves Hot Walkers

To Him who loved us and washed us from our sins in His own blood, and has made us kings and priests to His God and Father, to Him be glory and dominion forever and ever. Amen. Revelation 1:5-6

Just about everybody who works on the back-side of a race track has "walked hots" at one time or another. While the hot walker may be low man on the stable's totem pole, his, or her, job is one of great importance, an absolute necessity....horses need to be cooled out and taken down slow and easy once they've had a work.

While the hot walker may feel like he's at the bottom of the track pecking order, he can rest assured that he has a place in the heart of God that is no less important than the leading trainer, the leading jockey, or the president of the track. The Bible tells us that *God is no respecter* (shows no partiality) of persons.

Jesus said, *"He who is greatest among you shall be your servant."* Hence, it's evident that the Kingdom of God has a whole different value system than we have in the world.

One day, Jesus' twelve disciples got into an argument as to which one was the greatest—the boys had a little ego problem. Jesus was somewhat ticked, pulled them aside, and explained: *"If anyone desires to be first, he must be last of all and servant of all." And He took a little child and set him in the midst of them. And when He had taken him in His arms, He said to them, "Whoever receives one of these little children in My name receives Me; and whoever receives Me, receives not Me but Him who sent Me."*

Every member of the body of Christ is very important to God. Even if you're the skin on the bottom of the little toe, you're important in the Kingdom. Matter of fact, you peel the skin back from the bottom of that little toe, and you'll find your whole body slows down considerably.

Regardless of your position or status in the world, God looks at you as a precious new creation, a being made in His image, a bundle of tremendous potential upon whom He wants to heap His blessings of love, joy, and peace.

So, Mr. or Ms. Hot Walker, when you have Jesus in your heart, you are a king and a priest forever!
Sam Ed Spence

Acts 10:38   *Mark 9:33-37*
Matthew 23:11   *2 Corinthians 5:17*

Every member of the
body of Christ is very
important to God.

At the River's Edge
Russell Houston

The Unforced Rhythms of Grace

*"Are you tired? Worn out? Burned out on religion?
Come to me. Get away with me and you'll recover
your life. I'll show you how to take a real rest. Walk
with me and work with me - watch how I do it. Learn
the unforced rhythms of grace. I won't lay anything
heavy or ill-fitting on you. Keep company with me
and you'll learn to live freely and lightly."*

Matthew 11:28-30 The Message

Racing is a demanding life for a horse. While most race horses receive excellent care and attention, they must perform to a certain standard to remain in the racing stable. Otherwise, they're sold or "turned out to pasture."

Most religion is the same way. Religion says you must perform to be accepted by God, and you must continue to perform at a certain level to remain in His stable. But that's not what Jesus said. In the passage above from Matthew in *The Message* translation, Jesus makes it very clear that He's a great deal more interested in a *relationship* with us, rather than our *performance*.

In fact, He says that if we'll just keep close company with Him, He will show us how to accomplish far more in the midst of a rest, rather than in the performance pressures of religion and the world. Don't know about you, but that really whets my appetite to hobnob a bunch with this Jesus!

He's not saying to just lie down, get lazy and be some kind of flake. On the contrary, God's Word reveals that He has a very active, fulfilling, and productive plan for each of our lives. However, He is saying that the true and optimum productivity will come by our submitting to *His* working *through* us...turning our lives over to Him, to *rest* in Him.

That's what grace is all about; it's much more than "the unmerited favor of God," a definition generally accepted in Christian circles. Grace is the very *ability* of God—His power and wisdom that He makes available to every believer. God has given *natural* gifts to each of us, but they'll only take us so far. We generally come to the end of our own ability in rapid order; that's why we need to learn the *unforced rhythms of grace*—God's way of doing things—in order to enjoy that "free and light" lifestyle that Jesus has designed for us.

We don't have to *perform* to be in God's stable...just enjoy the green pastures and still waters where He leads us. *Sam Ed Spence*

> *Hebrews 4:1-11*   *Ephesians 2:10*
> *1 Timothy 6:18*   *Psalm 23:2*

Grace is the very ability of God—His power and wisdom that He makes available to every believer.

One Day at a Time

So do not worry or be anxious about tomorrow, for tomorrow will have worries and anxieties of its own. Sufficient for each day is its own trouble.
Matthew 6:34 AMP

Did you know that worry is a sin? It is, because worry is the opposite of faith. And the Bible says that *whatever is not of faith is sin.*

The main reason that God wants us to steer clear of sin is because it's so harmful to us. *The wages of sin are death.* Understand that it's not God doing the killing... it's the sin. God is totally on our side; in fact, He loves us so much that when we hurt, He hurts. If you're a parent, you can understand this. When my kidos were young and one of them would fall and get hurt, I hurt, too. Today, they're all grown up, but if one of them is going through a trial or tribulation, I hurt on the inside for them.

God is the same way about us; that's why He is never the author of *anything* but blessings in our lives. He knows that worry is a destroyer, that it is the "thief of peace." The only thing worry does is shorten your life. But Jesus said *"I have come that you might have life, and life more abundantly."*

So, you could say that God sent Jesus to the cross so that you and I don't have to worry anymore...about anything! This is not to say that we are to be careless and so care-free that we throw caution, good judgment and good stewardship to the wind...that's foolishness. But to worry, fret and stew over anyone or any situation only compounds the problem.

The antidote to worry is God's Word. Whatever your quandary, it's covered in the Word. Rather than ponder on the problem, get your Bible and start meditating the *answer.* Rest assured that God wants you to succeed, overcome and be a winner even more than you do.

Jesus said *that in this godless world we will always have some difficulties. "But don't sweat it, 'cause I've overcome the world!"* So let's take one day at a time...with Him, every day is a good one. *Sam Ed Spence*

Romans 14:23   *John 10:10*
Romans 6:23   *John 16:33*

The antidote to worry
is God's Word.

Kentucky Blue
Chuck DeHaan

Safe and Sound

For God did not send the Son into the world in order to judge (to reject, to condemn, to pass sentence on) the world, but that the world might find salvation and be made safe and sound through Him. John 3:17 AMP

Most all of us can quote John 3:16, *For God so loved the world that He gave His only begotten Son, so that whoever believes in Him shall not perish, but have everlasting life.*

A lot of folks have been born again on that one scripture; a lot of others have been saved by continuing on through the seventeenth verse (above), which explains the love nature of God and the M.O. of Jesus.

Some of us came to the Lord via "fire and brimstone messages" that literally scared the hell **out** of us. We believed these sermons because we were afraid not to! Later, we found out about the love of God and the fact that His salvation was much more than just fire insurance. I especially like the way the Amplified translation says it...*made safe and sound through Him.*

That speaks volumes to a horseman. First off, it means that Jesus is taking me into His stable to protect me, provide for me, and, meet all my needs...now that's really *safe!* Then comes the *sound* part, and it's big!

We all want our horses to be sound and to remain that way. The dictionary definition of the adjective, *sound,* is "to be free from defect, damage, or decay; whole and in good condition...normal and healthy; not weak, diseased, or impaired." Yep, that's how we want our running stock to be.

Better yet, that's how **we** can be, *through Him.* And He's not just talking about the life hereafter, that "sweet by-and-by" when we get to Heaven. The salvation He obtained for us at the cross provided safety and sound-ness for us in the "dirty-rotten now-and-now" of **this** world!

The key is *through Him.* It's not in our own strength, ability or goodness that we are made safe and sound. Rather, it is when we invite Jesus into our heart, sub-mit our life to Him, believe His Word, and walk in His commandments to love God and love one another... that's when this incredible safety and soundness mani-fests in the race of life. *Sam Ed Spence*

Romans 5:8   *3 John 2*
Luke 9:56   *Ephesians 2:8, 9*
1 John 4:18

The salvation He obtained
for us at the cross provided
safety and soundness for us
in the "dirty-rotten now-
and-now" of this world!

God's not the Problem

Let no one say when he is tempted, I am tempted from God; for God is incapable of being tempted by [what is] evil and He Himself tempts no one. James 1:13 AMP

Walking down a shedrow one morning, I came across Tracy, a seasoned jockey who had taken a spill a few days earlier. He had fractured a couple of bones in his wrist, which was now in a cast. "How's it doing," I inquired, pointing to the small cast.

"Great," replied Tracy. "No pain at all; Doc says I'll be back riding in just a few weeks. And, Chap, I know exactly why God had this happen to me. I've had some real quality time to spend with my 12-year-old daughter the past days that I probably wouldn't have had otherwise."

I forced back a frown, then motioned for Tracy to join me at a nearby empty tack room where we could have a little privacy to visit more. "Let me ask you a question, Tracy," I began, "would you break one of your daughter's wrists to make her do something?"

"Why heck no, Chaplain. I love her too much to do anything like that!" I smiled, but didn't reply, letting Tracy's own words sink into his think tank.

In a few moments, he returned the smile and said, "I see what you mean, Chap. You're saying God didn't have anything to do with my spill...I think I remember now you saying something about 'God not being the problem' in a jocks' devotion."

"That's exactly right, Tracy. God loves you even more than you love that beautiful daughter of yours, and He's not about to do anything that would cause you harm, loss, injury or sickness. That would absolutely be *against* His word and His nature. Jesus said He came to give us life more abundantly, but it's the thief who comes to kill, steal, and destroy. God's into blessings, not the hurting business."

"I see that, Chaplain, but there sure was some good that came out of this," replied the jockey, holding up his cast-bound wrist.

"That's because God is mighty good at turning lemons into lemonade," I replied. "Just look at us...we were pure lemons straight off sin's assembly line until Jesus came into our hearts and put His spirit on the inside of us. Even then, He didn't force Himself on us, but left the decision to accept Him totally up to us.

"Now, let's pray, Tracy, and believe God for a supernatural, rapid healing on that wrist...and you can still have plenty of quality time with your family...it's all up to you." *Sam Ed Spence*

1 John 4:7-10	Matthew 8:17
John 10:10	1 Peter 2:24

"That's because God is mighty good at turning lemons into lemonade..."

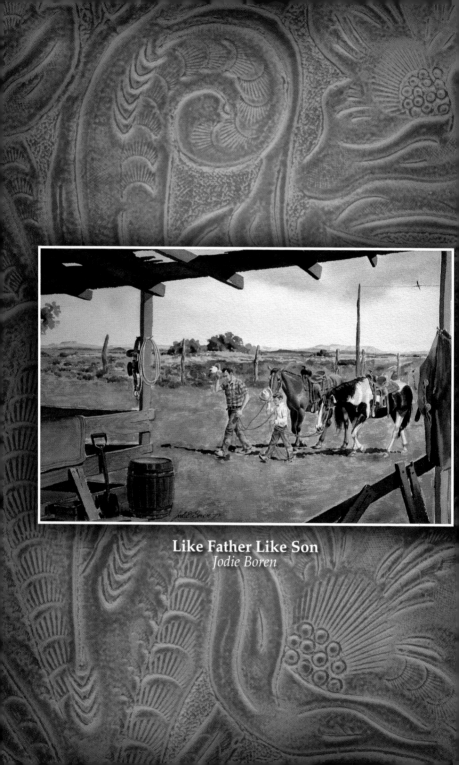

Like Father Like Son
Jodie Boren

Just Like Dad

"Anyone who has seen me has seen the Father...I am in the Father and the Father is in me. The words I say are not my own, but my Father who lives in me does his work through me." John 14:9-10 NLT

As a boy growing up on ranches in central Texas, I learned - or tried - to emulate my Dad in most everything. He was my first hero.

Dad taught me how to ride, rope, cut cattle, doctor wormies, build fences, fix water gaps...just about anything there was to do around stock or on the ranch. Taught me a lot of other things, too...about the importance of sticking to my word, finishing what I started, respecting elders, and putting in a full day's work. I really don't remember him preaching very much to me - he simply taught by example. Without realizing it, I picked up many of his traits. Even today, I catch myself doing some little quirk or habit, and the thought suddenly comes to me, "That's just how Dad did it."

At the last supper, Jesus astounded His disciples when He told them that He only spoke what the Father told Him, and everything He did was through the power of His Father. In fact, He answered the questioning Philip with the bold statement, *"If you've seen Me, you've seen the Father!"* Even though Jesus was one hundred per cent man, just like you and me, He was the "spittin' image" of His heavenly Father in all that He said and did...He had a mighty good role model.

So, if you ever have a question about the nature of God, or how He feels about a particular subject, or how He would handle a certain situation, just go to the Gospels (Matthew, Mark, Luke and John) and read what Jesus said and did...as well as what He *didn't* do.

You will find that Jesus never killed anyone, never put a sickness or disease on anyone, never made anyone destitute...never harmed anyone in any fashion. Instead, He raised people from the dead, healed the sick and diseased, gave to the poor, and blessed everyone who came to Him in faith.

The Bible tells us that Jesus is t*he same yesterday, today, and forever.* He's still doing the same things He always did...just like Dad. *Sam Ed Spence*

> *John 14:6-11* *Luke 7:21-23*
> *Colossians 1:15* *Hebrews 13:8*

"If you've seen me,
you've seen the father!"

The Almost-Too-Good-to-Be-True News

But He was wounded for our transgressions, He was bruised for our guilt and iniquities; the chastisement [needed to obtain] peace and well-being for us was upon Him, and with the stripes [that wounded] Him we are healed and made whole. Isaiah 53:5 AMP

I recently heard a Bible scholar explain that the best translation for the word, gospel, (referred to in most translations as "good news") is *almost-too-good-to-be-true news.* The fact that Jesus Christ died for our sins (actually *became* our sin) and paved the way for us to spend eternity with God is, in itself, mighty good news.

But when you delve into all that Jesus accomplished for us at the cross for our lives here on earth...well, that's when it gets *almost too good to be true!* Yet it is, because God can't lie. His Word is truth.

Hundreds of years before Jesus came to the earth, the prophet Isaiah spoke about much of what God's Son would purchase for us at Calvary. Isaiah's fifty-third chapter outlines the following:

1. Jesus was wounded and crushed for our sins; He bore all our sins so that we could be *righteous* (have a right standing with God) in this life.

2. Jesus was chastised (beaten) for our *peace.*
This is not peace as the world calls peace; this
is peace with God, just as the angels announced
to the shepherds at Jesus' birth: "peace on earth,
good will toward men." God's not upset with
us in any fashion, because the sacrifice of Jesus
satisfied all His wrath.
3. Because of the stripes that Jesus took, we are
healed and healthy.

"That's all fine and well," someone will say, "but why
do I feel so *unrighteous* at times? Why do I have so
many *non-peaceful* days? And why am I suffering from
diabetes, arthritis, heart trouble, etc., etc.,?"

The best answer to those questions comes in verse one:
"Who has believed (trusted in, relied upon, and clung
to) our message [of that which was revealed to us]?
(Isaiah 53:1 AMP) Jesus said that *all things are possible
to him that believes.*" (Mark 9:23)

The same faith we used to believe that Jesus is the Son
of God...the same faith by which we invited Him into
our hearts as our personal Savior...that's the same faith
we must use to receive our righteousness, our peace,
and our health...all of which was provided by Jesus at
the cross.

For good measure, let's throw in 2 Corinthians 8:9 AMP
...though He was so very rich, yet for your sakes He became

[so very] poor, in order that by His poverty you might become enriched (abundantly supplied).

"Why, Chaplain, that's just too good to be true!"

But it is! *Sam Ed Spence*

    2 Corinthians 5:21   *Mark 9:23*
    Isaiah 53:1 AMP   *2 Corinthians 8:9 AMP*

...that's the same faith we must use to receive our righteousness, our peace, and our health...

Who'll Go to the Lead
Tom Chapman

Throwing a Full Cross

And when He (Jesus) had called the people to Himself, with His disciples also, He said to them, "Whoever desires to come after Me let him deny himself, and take up his cross and follow Me." Mark 8:34

If you're an exercise rider or a jockey, you already know something about taking up a cross. And you well know the difference between a half cross and a full cross. Grasping the reins and crossing them so that one hand can hold them is fine for horses that don't pull hard and constantly try to run away. A half cross is also fine when you're breezing a horse or riding a race. Actually, the half cross is necessary, because it frees up your other hand to use the whip or help hand ride.

But if you've got a tough horse that wants to run off, and you need all the strength possible to restrain it, you need to throw that *full cross.* It gives you far more power and leverage. On a strong racehorse wanting to run off, you have to have that full cross.

It's the same way with the cross on which Jesus shed His blood for you. We can take a half cross and breeze through life in a full run. Yet, just as we know this would be disastrous to the health and training of a racehorse to let it run all-out all the time, it is also

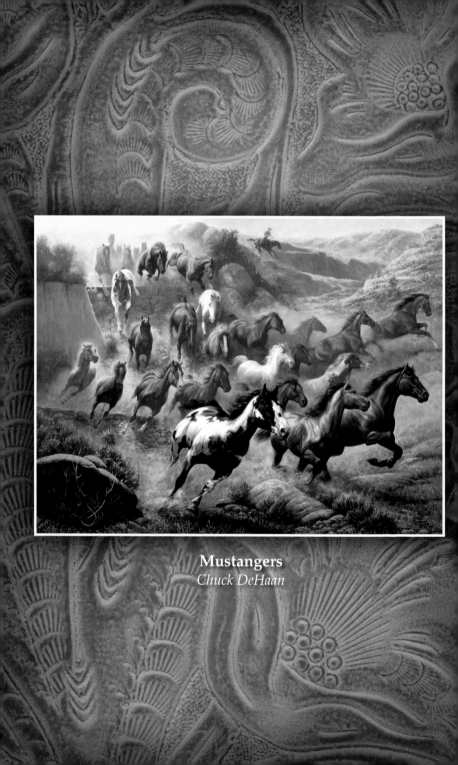

Mustangers
Chuck DeHaan

Running with the Herd

Oh, the joys of those who do not follow the advice of the wicked, or stand around with sinners, or join in with scoffers. Psalm 1:1 NLT

There's the story of a fellow who bought a couple of wild mustangs with the idea of eventually making riding horses out of them. This man also owned a gentle old pony horse that he'd had for years, and he decided to turn the mustangs in with the old horse in a small pasture near the house. His plan was for the pony horse to gentle down the wild horses to where he could easily catch them.

But the plan backfired. The longer the pony horse ran with the mustangs, the more he became like *them*, even to the point that the man could hardly catch his old horse.

The lesson here is to be very selective of the company you keep. This is especially true for the new believer. Many times when we come to Christ, we are still surrounded by friends and/or family who have not had that born-again experience. In fact, they may consider you a little strange, now that you've "got religion." That's okay. Keep loving and praying for them, but don't cut yourself loose and keep running in the pasture with them. Give the Holy Spirit free rein to guide and direct you in the company you keep and the places you go.

Make it a priority to surround yourself with believers, and stay immersed in God's Word. That's why the writer of Hebrews said to *not neglect our meeting together, as some people do, but encourage and warn each other...* what we call "going to church" - Bible studies, prayer meetings, and most important, that daily time you spend in the Word, communing with the Lord.

God does not call us to be hermits or loners. In fact, God's Word indicates that He does not often remove us from whatever situation we were in when we became a believer; that is, He usually wants us to stay right where we are and be a witness for Christ to those around us. But being a witness does not entail continuing to live a reckless lifestyle with the old cronies some of us were used to running with. We're not judging or condemning those old friends; we're simply saying a polite "no" to the invitations to the *wild life.*

Remember, we want to remain as that gentle pony horse...always easy to catch—responsive to the Master's beckoning call. *Sam Ed Spence*

2 Corinthians 6:14   *Hebrews 10:25*
Ephesians 5:6, 7   *1 Corinthians 7:20-24*

Make it a priority to surround yourself with believers, and stay immersed in God's Word.

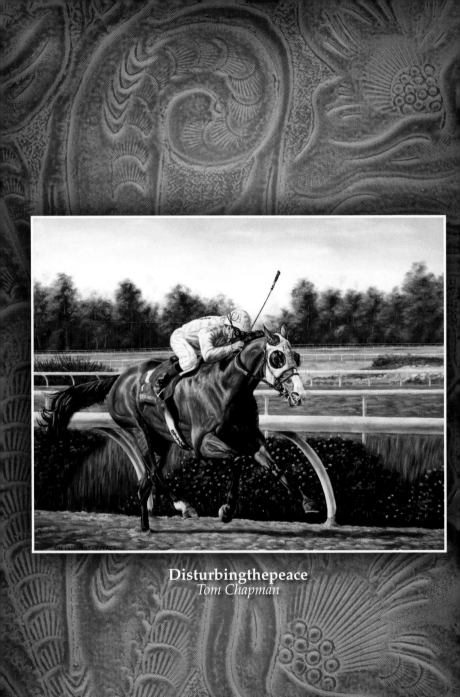

Disturbingthepeace
Tom Chapman

Blinkers On

Do not fret or have any anxiety about anything, but in every circumstance and in everything, by prayer and petition (definite requests), with thanksgiving, continue to make your wants known to God.

Philippians 4:6 AMP

During a race, some horses are easily distracted by what's going on around them. They get to paying too much attention to the crowd, the rail, or horses near them rather than their rider and the business of winning the race. Such horses are usually prime candidates for blinkers.

Most of us need blinkers, too. We can get easily distracted in the race of life by circumstances, temptations, cares of this world, and a whole bevy of *unbelief* that can keep us from winning the prize. The writer of Hebrews said we must strip off every distraction that slows us down and run with endurance the race that God has set before us.

So, what kind of blinkers do we put on?...*The Word of God!*

For example, let's say that you've set a personal goal to come out of debt - to be financially free. Then, suddenly, the bottom falls out. The transmission goes out of your pickup just as the warranty expires, your best pony horse colics and runs up a big vet bill, and you get a notice from the IRS that you underpaid last year's taxes...how's that for distractions?

Instead of throwing up your hands in despair and yelling "I can't do this - there's no way I'll ever get out of debt!"...put your *blinkers* on. Go to God's Word and get the answer to your situation, i.e., *My God shall supply all my needs according to His riches in glory by Christ Jesus* (Philippians 4:19); *I will owe no man anything but to love one another* (Romans 13:8); *I can do all things through Christ who strengthens me* (Philippians 4:13). There are many other promises of God that you can apply. The main thing is to get His Word established in your heart... get your eyes off the *problem* and keep them on the *answer.*

Once you've got your blinkers strapped on tight, then take some more of the Apostle Paul's advice to the Philippians: *Be anxious for nothing, but in everything by prayer and supplication, with thanksgiving, let your requests be made known to God* (Philippians 4:6).

Paul said we should present our requests *with thanksgiving.* No, this is not a formula on how to cajole God into answering our prayer. The thanksgiving comes because you are confident that He has already made provision for your success. You already have everything that pertains to life and godliness; you have all of God's power and resources in you - everything you need for personal victory. You're thankful because you recognize and acknowledge what you've *already* been given...thank You, Lord, for the blinkers. *Sam Ed Spence*

Hebrews 12:1 NLT
Romans 12:2

So, what kind of blinkers do we put on?...
THE Word of God!

The Power of Words

*Death and life are in the power of the tongue, and
those who love it will eat its fruit.*
Proverbs 18:21

Just before I got to the end of a shedrow on one of
my morning rounds, a string of expletives erupted
from the other side that would have made a sailor
blush. As I rounded the corner stall, the author of the
statements - a trainer friend of mine - looked up in
surprise. "Gosh, Chap, I'm sorry...I didn't know you
were around!"

I laughed and replied, "Aw, Frank (fictitious name),
that's okay...I'm not the one you have to answer to any-
how." Then I added (with the most non-condemning
grin and tone of voice I could muster up), "But Jesus
did say one time that *from the abundance of the heart, the
mouth speaks*...so I reckon we sorta know what's in your
heart, don't we!"

Frank chewed on that for a few moments, then replied,
"Man alive, Chap, you're being pretty hard on me!"

"No, partner, I don't mean to condemn you at all; I just
want to help you," I said. "You're exactly the way I
was some years back before I began to understand *the
power of words.* You see, that young horse you got upset

at over there is *not* going to have his plight improved by what you said about him; in fact, he's going to have a lot tougher row to hoe now than before you came down on him...all because of the power of the words we speak."

That really got Frank's attention, and he wanted to know more. I explained to him that God used words - *faith-filled* words - to form all of creation. In Genesis we read, *And God said, "let there be light"...And God said... And God said...*Then He made man in His image and gave him the power to use *words* to oversee and run the whole earth. It was the **power to speak** that gave Adam dominion over all the other creatures.

The words you and I speak are mighty important. Another Proverb says *"You are snared by the words of your mouth; you are taken by the words of your mouth.* Not only do our words reflect what we believe, they actually create an environment of faith, or an atmosphere of doubt. Think about it...your words can create an environment of faith, not only for your life, but also for the lives of others...including your horses!

Words paint pictures...pictures of defeat, or victory. Speak the devil's words, and doubt, fear and despair result. Speak God's Word, and the result is faith, hope and love.

Frank decided real quick he wanted to "tear up the

canvas" he had begun to paint of his young racing prospect...and start over with some faith-filled words of blessings. *Sam Ed Spence*

Matthew 12:34   Proverbs 13:3
Genesis 1:3, 6, 9, 11, 14, 20, 24, 26   Proverbs 6:2
Matthew 15:11

It was the power to speak that gave Adam dominion over all the other creatures.

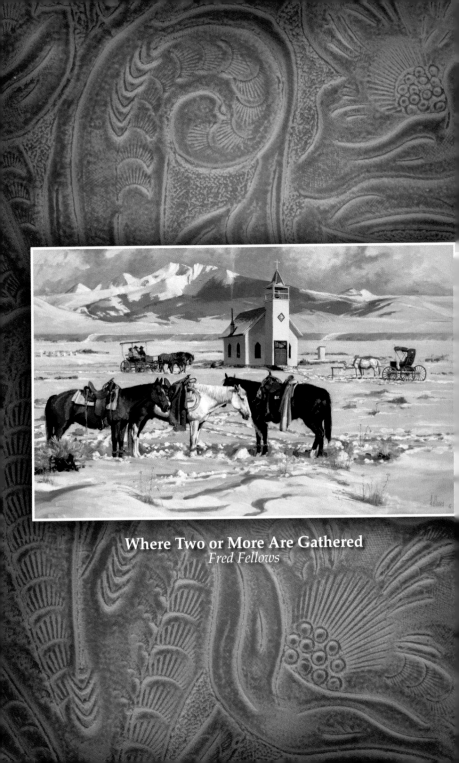

Where Two or More Are Gathered
Fred Fellows

Just a Closer Walk

*Listen for God's voice in everything you do, every-
where you go; he's the one who will keep you on track.*
Proverbs 3:6 The Message

ust a Closer Walk with Thee" has always been one
of my favorite hymns. One morning I was quietly
humming this old tune to myself as I got dressed to go
to the track..."just a closer walk with thee, grant it Jesus
is my plea..." As the word, "plea," rolled off my lips, I
very distinctly heard the Lord say, *"It can be just as close
as you want it to be."*

He got my full attention with that statement, and as I
began to meditate on it, I realized that the only limit-
ing factor to a *closer walk* was me. God is fully willing,
even very desirous, of a mighty *tight* relationship with
each one of His children...you and I are no exceptions.

But a most interesting trait of our Father is that He will
never *force* Himself on us. In fact, I'm not sure that the
word, *force*, is even in God's vocabulary. God is love,
and according to 1 Corinthians 13, God's kind of love
is patient, kind, never overbearing, yet never gives up
and never fails. Yes, the Holy Spirit will bring strong
conviction to your heart, but the final decision is always yours; you will never be *forced* by God nor have
your personal will violated by Him.

Getting back to that closer walk, the writer of Hebrews tells us that *God rewards those who diligently seek Him.* That tells me I have a very important part to play in this relationship with my Creator. It's up to *me* to seek *Him.* Not that He's hard to locate; after all, He promised in His Word that He would never leave us nor forsake us. In fact, He makes His home right on the inside of us. Yet, it seems that His M.O. is to never barge-in or horn-in on us, but rather to manifest by invitation only...i.e., prayer, meditation or quiet time.

Jesus said, *"Ask, and it shall be given you; seek and you shall find; knock, and it shall be opened to you."* Appears to me God is making Himself readily available, but He has put the ball in our court—*you* ask, *you* seek, *you* knock. Notice, however, He did not say, "you perform, you do, or you earn." No, indeed, this relationship comes about by faith - simply by your believing that He has already accepted you, forgiven you, and loves you unconditionally.

So, unlike the old hymn, we really don't have to *plea* for a closer walk; we simply invite, receive, and enjoy it...and He keeps us right on track. What a deal!

Sam Ed Spence

1 John 4:8   *Hebrews 13:5*
1 Corinthians 13:4-8   *Matthew 7:7*
Hebrews 11:6   *John 14:23*

God is fully willing, even very desirous, of a mighty tight relationship with each one of His children...

God's Not Holding Out

Now to Him, Who, by (in consequence of) the [action of His] power that is at work within us, is able to [carry out His purpose and] do superabundantly, far over and above all that we [dare] ask or think - infinitely beyond our highest prayers, desires, thoughts, hopes or dreams-Ephesians 3:20 AMP

Recently I had someone in my office who was pretty peeved at God. This person had prayed about a situation in his life, but it hadn't worked out according to the way he thought it should. He felt that God had let him down.

I certainly didn't know all the details of this man's life and situation, but one thing I *did* know - God didn't fail, nor was He holding out on my friend. Either the prayer was not *in faith*, or God was doing something even better than my friend could see at the present time.

A lot of times, we're "hoping and praying," rather than praying and believing. Jesus said in Mark 11:24, *"Therefore I tell you, whatever you ask for in prayer, believe that you have received it, and it shall be yours."* That's praying *in faith.*

So often we voice a prayer to God, and then we come with a statement like, "Well, I sure *hope* that works."

Actually, that's absolute double-mindedness, and the Apostle James said *a double-minded man can receive nothing from God.*

Before we ever pray, we need to get it settled in our hearts that we're praying God's will and that He is agreeable, (even anxious) to meet our need. Then we can come boldly into the throne of grace and receive our need met.

When it comes to finding God's will in a matter, the best place to start is in His Word. For example, 3 John 2 says, *"Beloved, I pray that you may prosper in every way and [that your body] may keep well, even as [I know} your soul keeps well and prospers." AMP* That one scripture tells us God's will in a great portion of our lives - prosperity, health, and wholeness in our mind and emotions. Sometimes it's good to meditate (chew on) a scripture like this for a spell before you ever pray. Then you can pray in faith, believing.

A couple of weeks later, my friend walked back into the office with a grin on his face as big as Dallas. "You know that deal I was praying about the other day," he recalled, "well, this morning I had an even better deal work out for me...I reckon God knew what He was doing!"

I laughed and shared one of my favorite scriptures with him: *"God can do anything, you know - far more than you could ever imagine or guess or request in your wildest dreams!"* (Ephesians 3:20 The Message)

God is on your side. He's not holding out on you.
Sam Ed Spence

Mark 11:24 NIV	*Romans 12:2*
James 1:6-8	*Hebrews 4:16*

When it comes to finding God's will in a matter, the best place to start is in His Word.

Stage to Deadwood
Chuck DeHaan

Horses and Chariots

*Some trust in and boast of chariots and some of horses,
but we will trust in and boast of the name of the
Lord our God.* Psalm 20:7 AMP

The eighteenth chapter of Luke records the incident
of a very wealthy young man questioning Jesus
about how to receive eternal life. A slight bit cocky, the
fellow told Jesus that he had kept all the commandments since he was a small boy.

Jesus, however, took the wind out of his sails when He
told him, *"There is still one thing you lack. Sell all you have
and give the money to the poor, and you will have treasure in
heaven. Then come follow me."* The Bible says this young
man's countenance went straight south, because he
had great riches.

As the dejected young fellow walked away, Jesus said
something that also astounded his disciples: *"How hard
it is for rich people to get into the kingdom of God!"*

"Then who in the world can be saved? asked Peter, who
himself had been made independently wealthy by that
boat-sinking load of fish he caught after loaning his
vessel to Jesus for a preaching platform. Jesus went on
to explain that no man can save himself, but with God,
any man can be saved, even the very rich...provided
they place their trust in God rather than in their
great wealth.

Just like the rich young man, many people of great means put their trust in the riches, rather than in their Creator. Few realize that it is God who gives them the grace and ability to get wealth in the first place. Had this young man truly had a knowledge of God's Word, he would have known that Jesus was not placing a "call to poverty" on him. Quite the contrary, Proverbs says that *"If you help the poor, you are lending to the Lord - and he will repay you!"* And the Lord is no slacker; He repays thirty, sixty and a hundredfold. That young fellow turned down the opportunity to become rich beyond his fondest dreams, besides refusing an offer to be one of Jesus' right hand men.

Many of us grew up in an environment that taught us to place our trust in material things - money, our own abilities, our jobs, influence with people, etc. We had little idea that God had a wonderful plan for our lives that entailed total faith and trust in Him. He certainly expects us to be good stewards of all we have, but the life of trust in God brings riches of joy, peace and ful-fillment that material wealth can never touch.

God wants you to have good horses and fine vehicles... just don't put your trust in them...place your trust in the Lord Jesus Christ. *Sam Ed Spence*

Luke 18:18-30 NLT   *Proverbs 19:17 NLT*
Luke 5:1-10   *Proverbs 3:5*
Deuteronomy 8:18

Few realize that it is God who gives them the grace and ability to get wealth in the first place.

Keeping on Track

Trust God from the bottom of your heart; don't try to figure out everything on your own. Listen for GOD's voice in everything you do, everywhere you go; he's the one who will keep you on track.

Proverbs 3:5, 6 The Message

Being a rather simple, uncomplicated person, I find tremendous comfort in the proverb above. I love it that I don't have to figure out complicated situations or problems. I can simply trust my Father to handle the twisters and mind bogglers; all I have to do is tune in to the Holy Spirit and follow His lead.

The key word in all this is **trust**...trust in a heavenly Father Who loves you unconditionally and has your very best interests at heart. He is **not** going to lead you down the primrose lane or get you in a passel of problems to "teach you something" or "build your faith." That is totally against the nature of God and the Word of God...it's just not His M.O.

On the other hand, He may instruct you to do something that really comes against your flesh, your *reasoning* mind and *your* normal mode of operation. If you are really in doubt that the instruction came from God, ask Him for confirmation...or simply, "Lord, would you please say that again?" (You probably heard it loud and clear the first time - your flesh just didn't *want* to hear it!)

Two character flaws often bring us up short in the *trusting-God* arena: Pride and unworthiness. Pride says, "I don't need God in this; I can handle it myself... besides, trusting God in *everything* is pretty wimpy." Unworthiness says, "I'm really not a good enough Christian to ask God for this." Unworthiness is a subtle form of self-righteousness, as opposed to faith-righteousness (trusting in the shed blood of Jesus Christ for our right-standing with God).

Both pride and unworthiness are deceptions, trust-stealers that will pull you off the track that God has designed for you to run on. You can shuck both of these thieves by renewing your mind with God's Word and spending quality *quiet time* with the Holy Spirit. Learn to listen for God's voice in the little things; then you'll find it much easier when the biggies show up. And always remember, He's there for you in *everything* you do, *everywhere* you go. Trust Him. *Sam Ed Spence*

John 10:3   *Job 35:12, 13*
Psalm 37:3, 23   *Philippians 3:9*

...trust in a heavenly Father
Who loves you unconditionally
and has your very best
interests at heart.

Counting His Blessings
Jack Sorenson

Forget Not All His Benefits

Bless the LORD, O my soul, and forget not all His benefits:
Who forgives all your iniquities, who heals all your diseases,
who redeems your life from destruction, who crowns you
with lovingkindness and tender mercies, who satisfies your
mouth with good things, so that your youth is renewed like
the eagle's. Psalm 103:2-5

Imagine having a sure-fire, multiple-stakes winner in your barn, all prepped, ready to run... but you keep forgetting to go to the entry booth with him!

"That's ridiculous," you say, "nobody's that stupid!" Yes, it would be rather difficult to find someone in racing who had that caliber of horse and yet was so ab-sent-mined they never ran him. Not nearly so difficult is it to find a Christian who has forgotten the benefits that Jesus Christ has provided for us.

In the scripture above, the psalmist David had a good handle on God's benefits for the believer; yet, even those benefits don't encompass all that Jesus obtained for you and me via the cross. Far too often we lose sight of what is available—indeed, what truly *belongs* to us—as children of God. Peace, prosperity, protection and provision were all purchased when Jesus pulled off the "big exchange" for us and paid the supreme sac-rifice at Calvary.

To experience those benefits, however, one must write them on the tablets of his heart. God's Word must become more real to you than any circumstance, any problem, any sin or any shortfall in your life. Sometimes the trials and tribulations we experience can cloud our *memory* of what God's Word says about us. That's why we must have those benefits transferred from our *mind* to our *heart*...by meditating the Word and spending daily time with the Father.

All His benefits are yours...and don't you forget it!
Sam Ed Spence

Isaiah 53:4-5   *Proverbs 3:1-4*
Ephesians 1:3-12   *2 Corinthians 8:9*
Luke 15:31   *Joshua 1:8*

Peace, prosperity, protection and provision were all purchased when Jesus pulled off the "big exchange" for us and paid the supreme sacrifice at Calvary.

Daily Oats
Kay Griffith

Past—Gone—Forgotten

Therefore, if anyone is in Christ, he is a new creation; old things have passed away; behold, all things have become new. 2 Corinthians 5:17

She walked into my office with a face longer than California. That, plus the first words out of her mouth, let me know that here was a very unhappy camper. An exercise rider who had been saved in a track chapel service about a year earlier, she was finding very little joy in her salvation.

In a very few minutes I knew why: Her past life was haunting her. "Get over it...put it behind you," I said, "God has!"

"What do you mean?" she retorted, obviously surprised and a little hurt by my bluntness.

"What I mean is, God has not only totally forgiven you, He has completely *forgotten* about all those shortcomings. There's no record anywhere in Heaven of even one of them. The blood of Jesus washed them right out of existence. He didn't just cover them; he eradicated them."

"But I just can't see how God could really love the kind of person I am, what with all the junk I've done."

"Correction: the kind of person you *were*. Truth is, He loved you even then, but when you accepted Jesus as your Savior, He gave you a new heart and put His Spirit within you - God made you a brand new creature. Remember all that joy and peace you felt when you first got saved?"

"Yeah, what happened to that?"

"In a nutshell, you kept seeing and thinking the way *you* see you, rather than renewing your mind to the way *God* sees and feels about you. He sees you totally righteous, a new creature with His complete approval. And you have to start thinking *His* way.

"This is why the Apostle Paul exhorted the Ephesians to *"no longer walk as the rest of the Gentiles walk, in the futility of their mind.* He told the Romans to *be transformed by the renewing of your mind.* He instructed the Corinthians to *"cast down imaginations (arguments), and every high thing that exalts itself against the knowledge of God, bringing every thought into captivity to the obedience of Christ."*

"So shape up, girl; get rid of that "stinkin' thinkin'" and start acting like that new creature you are."

For a long moment, the exercise rider stared at me like a calf at a new gate. "God really feels that way about me, huh? Well, I reckon I'll have another go at it."

Sam Ed Spence

Isaiah 43:25   *Romans 12:2*
Revelation 1:5   *2 Corinthians 10:4,5 AMP*
Ephesians 4:17   *Psalm 103:12*

He sees you totally righteous, a new creature with His complete approval.

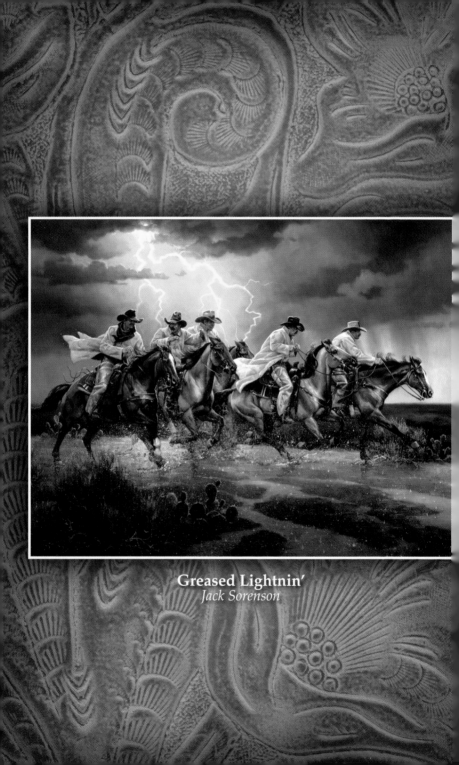

Greased Lightnin'
Jack Sorenson

Preparing for the Storm

*I have told you these things, so that in Me you may
have [perfect] peace and confidence. In the world you
have tribulation and trials and distress and frustration; but be of good cheer [take courage; be confident,
certain, undaunted]! For I have overcome the world. [I
have deprived it of power to harm you and have con-
quered it for you.] John 16:33 AMP*

One of the distinguishing features of my Grand-
father's blackland farm in central Texas was the
storm cellar which sat in the edge of the cotton field
immediately in front of the house. The storm cellar
was almost completely underground, save a wooden
ground-level door that opened to the stairs, and a small
ventilator at the top to receive fresh air. Whenever a
dark cloud blew up or a potential storm headed our
way, Granddad herded us to the storm cellar. He was
taking no chances on any of us being blown away.

When I was about 12, Granddad dug a big hole and
put in a new storm cellar in the field just north of the
house; this one had eight-inch-thick concrete walls and
ceiling. I think that took place in the early fifties right
after a devastating killer tornado had swept through
downtown Waco, about 25 miles from the farm. Looking back, that storm cellar was about as close as you
could get to a bomb shelter in central Texas. Granddad

was ready for any storm that might come our way.

In the scripture above, Jesus is preparing us for the storms of life - tribulation, trials, distress and frustration; we're all going to have them - it's a fact of life. But Jesus Christ is our storm cellar. He overcame the world's system, lived a sinless life, then paid the supreme price for our sins at the cross. In his letter to the Colossians, the Apostle Paul confirms that Jesus stripped Satan and his forces in this world of the power to condemn and destroy us.

When we are born again, we are *in* Jesus...we enter into our storm cellar. When the stormy circumstances of life blow in, we should never get into fear or bow our knee to those various tribulations - that's exactly what the devil is trying to get us to do. Instead, we should go straight to God's Word, claim it as our own (which it is), then **speak** that Word **to** the circumstances. And while you're at it, speak that same Word to Satan, reminding him that he is a defeated foe, stripped of his power and authority. Remember, Jesus said that the devil is a liar and there's no truth in him. Satan wants us to put more faith in the circumstances (the problem) than we put in God's Word; his goal is to make us more *world-oriented* rather than *Word-oriented*.

There are dozens of scriptures throughout the epistles of the New Testament that refer to us being *in* Christ, *in* Jesus or *in* Him. In his letter to the Ephesians, Apostle

Paul says *In Him* we have redemption through His blood, the forgiveness of sins, according to the riches of His grace... *In Him* also we have obtained an inheritance, being predestined according to the purpose of Him who works all things according to the counsel of His will.

Jesus is our storm cellar. Get that in your heart, and no ill wind of circumstance can have its way with you.
Sam Ed Spence

Colossians 2:14, 15   John 8:44
Ephesians 1:7, 11   Matthew 4:4, 7, 10

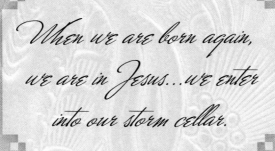

When we are born again, we are in Jesus...we enter into our storm cellar.

The Giver

"Give away your life; you'll find life given back, but not merely given back - given back with bonus and blessing. Giving, not getting, is the way. Generosity begets generosity." Luke 6:38 The Message

Jesus often instructs us to do exactly opposite of our natural tendencies and certainly contrary to what the world tells us.

Most of us grew up learning to take care of "number one" and to let everyone else fend for themselves. As children, we had to be *taught* to share our toys, food, time, and anything else we considered precious; sharing and giving is not the *natural* thing to do...we had to learn to be givers.

And we're still learning, especially when it comes to the type of giving that Jesus talked about in the passage above. Getting a handle on this type of giving is the very essence of life itself. Our heavenly Father set the pattern for us when He *gave* His Son, Jesus the Christ, so that you and I could be a part of His eternal family.

So is Jesus talking about you and me laying our lives down as human sacrifices just as He did at the cross? Not really. He is talking about investing our lives, our finances, time and talents in the lives of others...loving our neighbors as ourselves. He is talking about submitting our will to the will of the Father so that eternal purposes can be accomplished in the Kingdom through our giving.

Few incidents in life are more rewarding or exhilarating than having the Holy Spirit impress you to give to a particular person or area of need when you actually have some needs yourself. Whenever that happens, you'd better buckle up for a blessing! It's on the way! This is not some kind of "giving-to-get" Christian con game. Rather, it's God's system of meeting needs and blessing his children.

In 1 Kings of the Old Testament, we find a starving widow in drought-stricken Zarephath. She was about to use the last little bit of oil and corn meal she had to make a "final meal" for her and her son. The old prophet told her to make a cake for him instead. Reluctantly, she complied....only to find out that the corn meal barrel and the oil can just kept filling up. They never ran out...because she was obedient to give in the midst of her need.

Want to experience a big change in your life? Just spend a little time with the Holy Spirit and seek Him for opportunities to give of your life to others. As an old saint once proclaimed, "Cast your bread upon the waters, and hot biscuits will come back on every wave." *Sam Ed Spence*

Romans 12:2	*Luke 10:25-37*
John 3:16	*1 Kings 17:8-16*

Our heavenly Father set the pattern for us when He gave His son, Jesus the Christ...

Seabiscuit, an American Legend
Tom Chapman

All Heart

But the Lord said unto Samuel, "Look not on his countenance, or on the height of his stature; because I have refused him: for the Lord sees not as man sees; for man looks on the outward appearance, but the Lord looks on the heart." 1 Samuel 16:7

After Saul, the first king of Israel, royally messed up his kingdom, God instructed the prophet Samuel to go to the house of Jesse in Bethlehem, *"for I have provided Me a king among his sons."* Jesse brought out his eldest son, Eliab, who must have looked like an all-pro linebacker. Samuel said to himself, "I've got the new king right here before me.... somebody hand me my anointing oil!"

But God stopped Samuel short, and spoke the words above to him. In all, Jesse led seven great looking sons before Samuel, but God rejected them all. It was the youngest of the lot, little freckle-faced David that was God's pick. Jesse hadn't even bothered to bring him in from tending the sheep. But God knew his heart; hence, David was His choice.

I got my first horse when I was six-years-old. Tony wasn't much to look at, about 13 hands, a black and white Paint, probably part Shetland. But I could do anything on him—rope, work stock, gather horses; I even hazed on Tony for Dad when he would practice bull dogging. Tony always gave me everything he had...he was all heart.

Most everyone has seen one or two race horses like that —the kind that give you 100% every time they break from the gate. Seabiscuit was evidently one of those horses; not a lot to look at, but he had a mighty big heart. These horses have a way of winning *our* hearts.

Interestingly, God referred to David as a "man after My own heart." As you read the Psalms of David, you begin to see why he was God's pick to lead Israel. David sought God, he loved God, and—perhaps just as important—he trusted God. Hebrews says *Without faith it is impossible to please Him.* It was David's faith (his trust) that captured God's own heart.

While God loves each of us unconditionally, the key to being a real Father-pleaser is to trust Him with our lives by believing in our hearts what His Word says about us. *Sam Ed Spence*

1 Samuel 16:1	*Hebrews 11:6*
1 Samuel 13:14	*Psalm 37:4-8*

It was Davids faith
(his trust) that captured
God's own heart.

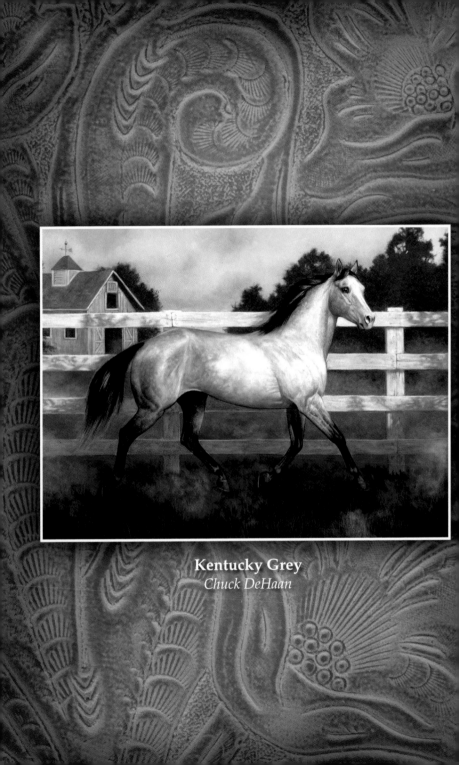

Kentucky Grey
Chuck DeHaan

All for His Glory

Let every detail in your lives - words, actions, whatever - be done in the name of the Master, Jesus, thanking God the Father every step of the way.
Colossians 3:17 The Message

God knew about you and planned your creation before He laid the foundations of the earth. You are not an accident. You were planned by God and created by Him for His pleasure and enjoyment.

Getting a handle on this truth - that you exist for the delight, purpose, and glory of God - should forever put to rest any problem you have had with dignity and self-worth. Keep in mind that God has chosen you to spend eternity with Him. As a child of God you are most significant, very important, to Him.

During a chapel service at the track one Sunday morning, I heard myself say, "There's a place in the heart of God that only you can satisfy." I knew that came straight from the Holy Spirit, and it made me realize that as a child of God, each of us brings pleasure to Father God like nothing else He has ever created. The Bible says *His unchanging plan has always been to adopt us into his own family by bringing us to himself through Jesus Christ. And this gave him great pleasure.*

Let the peace, joy, and comfort of being God's child so permeate your soul that you wake up in the morning thanking Him. Then let that spirit of praise carry through in every detail of your day, regardless of the conflicts, challenges, and contrary circumstances that come your way. Whether you're a hot walker, trainer, groom, or maintenance man, you can do your job with poise and dignity when you do it *"to the glory and praise of God." Sam Ed Spence*

Ephesians 1:4-5 NLT   *1 Thessalonians 5:18*
Jeremiah 29:11 AMP   *Philippians 1:9-11*
Psalm 8:5

"There's a place in the heart of God that only you can satisfy."

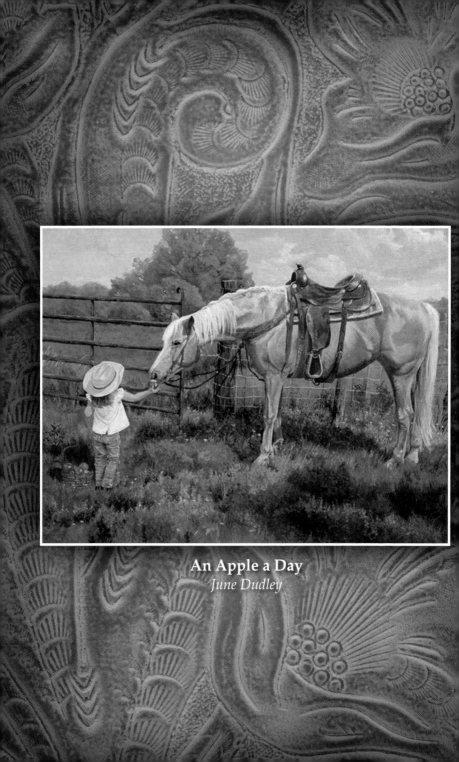

An Apple a Day
June Dudley

What a Friend!

A friend loves at all times, and a brother is born for adversity. Proverbs 17:17

Several years ago a team of psychologists conducted a survey in mental institutions across the country. They found a common denominator in over seventy per cent of all the patients interviewed: no best friends. Almost three-quarters of the people in the survey said they had no individual in their lives that they could call a *"best friend,"* someone they could trust, pour out their heart, and know that whatever they shared would remain confidential.

Almost one hundred per cent of those who admitted this lack felt they would not be in their present condition had a best friend existed in their past. How sad that no one had ever introduced these folks to the Lord Jesus Christ, the *friend that sticks closer than a brother.*

Almost as sad is the fact that many Christians go through life without knowing that Jesus wants to be their best friend. I did, for many years. Then, one day I was reading the Gospel of John where Jesus said, *"I no longer call you servants, because a master doesn't confide in his servants. Now you are my friends, since I have told you everything the Father told me."* Instantly, that scripture became very personal, and I knew that Jesus was more than my Creator, even more than my Savior; He was my very best buddy.

From then on, prayer time became more like *share* time...I began to share my innermost feelings and struggles, along with my joys and dreams. Amazingly, *He* began to share *secrets* with me—intimate, personal things—and I knew they were just between us.

The Bible says that God *is no respecter of persons.* In other words, He loves no one because of his position, title or accomplishments in this world. He loves each of us just the same, but that love is customized into a very personal relationship that is available for each of God's children. It's a best friend connection...just for you. *Sam Ed Spence*

> *Proverbs 17:17*   *John 15:15 NLT*
> *Proverbs 18:24*   *Acts 10:34*

...many Christians go through life without knowing that Jesus wants to be their best friend.

Prayer—A Two-way Street

The sacrifice of the wicked is an abomination to the Lord: but the prayer of the upright is His delight.
Proverbs 15:8

Most of us grew up thinking that prayer was something we did before we ate, went to bed, or used to get God's help in desperate situations. The Bible does tell us to *come boldly into the throne of grace in the time of need.* However, the Creator's *Condition Book* has a lot more to say about prayer than it being simply an avenue to solicit His assistance.

Possibly the best definition of prayer is simply "conversation with God." Couple this with the fact that God really desires to be your best friend, and prayer suddenly takes on a whole new meaning.

Think about a visit you've had with a real good friend. Most likely a lot of talking took place—both ways. You both talked, and you both listened. A conversation with God—prayer—should be no different. Regretfully, most of us have a *one-way-street* prayer life. We rattle off our want-list to God... "in Jesus name, Amen" - and we're outta the throne room and on our way. It seldom occurs to us that God may have some things He wants to share with us. He just might want to share the very answer to your prayer, some wisdom that meets your need immediately.

We simply need to slow down and tune in our *spiritual* ears to the Holy Spirit that lives on the inside of us—that *still, small voice* who spoke to Elijah. Seldom does God speak to us in an audible voice; rather He speaks to our heart with thoughts and impressions. We must develop a *hearing* heart and a *listening* prayer life. This comes primarily by 1) renewing our mind with God's Word, and 2) setting aside quality times for meditation and conversation with the Father.

The Holy Spirit, Who is always with us, is referred to in the Bible as our *Teacher,* our *Comforter,* and our *Advocate.* Those titles indicate He has much to say to us. We just need to learn to listen to His voice.

The Apostle Paul admonishes us to *pray without ceasing.* In other words, keep an on-going conversation with the Father - a conversation of speaking and listening; remember, that's the Lord's delight. *Sam Ed Spence*

> *Hebrews 4:16*   *1 Kings 19:12*
> *Proverbs 18:24*   *1 Thessalonians 5:17*
> *James 1:5*

We simply need to slow down and tune in our spiritual ears to the Holy Spirit...

Spooked
Chuck DeHaan

No Fear

For God has not given us a spirit of fear, but of power and of love and of a sound mind. 2 Timothy 1:7

Try to imagine what it would be like to have absolutely no fear in your life. No fear of harm coming to you, no fear of disease or bad health, no fear of lack of any kind...and absolutely no fear of death.

"Impossible," you say.

Not so, according to the Word of God. The Apostle John wrote *"There is no fear in love; but perfect love casts out fear.* He's talking about God's love for you and me. You see, because of what Jesus accomplished in His death and resurrection, we never have to fear being punished by God for our sins, failures and shortcomings. When Jesus, the perfect sacrifice, became our sin, He forever satisfied the wrath of God. Once we personally accept that sacrifice, we never have to fear judgment from God.

"But what about that Psalm that says *the fear of the Lord is the beginning of wisdom?"* someone will ask.

The best translation for the Hebrew word for fear (yirah) in the Old Testament is *reverence* or *awesome respect.* It's not a trembling, shaking-in-your-boots fear;

rather it is a deep, reverent appreciation for the "awe-someness" of our loving Creator.

As you begin to get a handle on the unconditional love that God has for you, all kinds of fear start to fade away. The Apostle Paul understood God's love. He said there was nothing on the earth, under the earth or in the heavens that could separate God's love from him. That's how Paul was able to confidently state, *"O death, where is your sting?"* Paul, who went through tremendous persecutions and tribulations, had fear for no person and no circumstance, because he had the love of God firmly embedded in his heart.

Look at King David in the Old Testament, who said in his 23rd Psalm, "though I walk *through the valley of the shadow of death, I will fear no evil..."* David had the Holy Spirit upon him, but he did not have Him living on the inside of him like you and I do as born-again believ-ers. We've got a better deal than David had, or that of Abraham, who was called "the friend of God."

Because of the unconditional love that God has for us in Christ Jesus, we don't have to fear anything. Not even failure. When we do come up short on some project or endeavor, we can simply use it as a learning experience, not something that throws us into a tailspin. Remember, God is not the author of fear; rather He gives us a sound mind of love, power, and self control. You don't have to be spooked by anything! *Sam Ed Spence*

> 1 John 4:18 Romans 8:38, 39
> Romans 5:8-11 1 Corinthians 15:55
> Psalm 111:10

Because of the unconditional love that God has for us in Christ Jesus, we don't have to fear anything.

Just an Ol' Cheap Claimer

Therefore if any person is [in-grafted] in Christ (the Messiah) he is a new creation (a new creature altogether); the old [previous moral and spiritual condition] has passed away. Behold, the fresh and new has come!

2 Corinthians 5:17

An ol' cheap claimer...that's what we were, you know, before God dropped that claim in the box some 2,000 years ago and claimed us as His own. The "claim box," of course, was the cross at Calvary, where Jesus paid a gargantuan price for us...far more that we were worth, except in God's eyes.

In the natural, we were a bunch of broke down, bog-spavined, shin-bucked, bowed, bleeders headed for the meat wagon. God wasn't fooled; He knew exactly what He was getting. Somehow, in His unfathomable love, He figured it was a good claim. I, for one, am mighty glad He did, and that Jesus agreed to go along with Him on the claim.

Unlike the racing world, however, where the horse has no choice, God leaves it totally up to us in regard to joining His stable. Even though He paid the full claim price, it's our choice to join Him, or to keep running for the devil.

Once we make the decision to run under Jesus' colors,

then comes the really great news about this whole race of life...that God, through the work of His head trainer, the Holy Spirit, has turned us into stakes runners. In fact, He looks at *each* of us as "the big horse" in His stable.

"Aw, come on now, Chaplain...you're going just a little too far with this thing...Me?...The big horse?" (I can hear the wheels turning as you're reading this.)

Problem is, too often we hang on to the "cheap claimer" mentality, and that's the way we see ourselves...just another "also ran." The real truth, however, is what God's Word says about us - not what we *feel* about ourselves.

For example, the Bible tells us that a believer in Christ is a *new creation*, with old things passed away and all things new. God has replaced your old stony heart with one of flesh (of feeling and goodness) and put His spirit on the inside of you. That spirit is one of love, and power, and a sound mind of discipline and self control. If this doesn't sound like you, it's only because you haven't lined your thinking up with how God sees you.

God does not look at us according to our natural bloodlines, conformation, or track record. He simply loves us, and He sees us through the shed blood of His son, which tattooed us with "approved."

You're no longer just an ol' cheap claimer saved by grace. You're the big horse headed for the winner's circle...you're a child of the living God, and all His promises are yours! *Sam Ed Spence*

Ephesians 2:1-5   *Ezekiel 11:19*
John 3:16   *2 Timothy 1:7*

Somehow, in His unfathomable love, He figured it was a good claim.

Tying the Knots in the Devil's Tail
George Phippen

The Defeated Foe

Then the Devil, who betrayed them, was thrown into the lake of fire that burns with sulfur, joining the beast and the false prophet. There they will be tormented day and night forever and ever. Revelation 20:10 NLT

Most all of us have prayed at one time or another: "Lord, get the devil off my back!" Actually, that's not a scriptural prayer. In fact, it's a prayer that God can't answer...because He has already answered it. The Bible says Jesus totally defeated the devil and all his cohorts when He went to the cross...*[God] disarmed the principalities and powers that were ranged against us and made a bold display and public example of them, in triumphing over them in Him and in it [the cross].*

When the Apostle Paul wrote the words, "made a bold display and public example of them," the Roman subjects at Colossae knew exactly what he was talking about. In those days, when a king or military leader defeated an opposing army, they would cut off the thumbs of the captured king or leader, so that he couldn't hold a sword. Then his big toes were severed, so that he was basically immobile; he was then led naked through the streets behind the chariot of the conquering king to show that he (the fallen leader) had no more power and was no longer a threat to the people.

Paul definitely got his point across to the Colossians that—in the spirit world—Satan had suffered a devastating defeat. It meant that the power which the first Adam had handed over to the devil in the Garden had been stripped away by the last Adam (Christ Jesus) and given back to every man, or woman, who would accept Jesus as their *King.*

Sometimes we give far too much credit to the devil. Paul and the other writers of the epistles actually devote very little space to Satan and his kingdom of darkness. They understood that the only real "power" the devil has is *deception*, which he attempts to use on everybody. He's done a pretty good "snow job" convincing many of us today that he still has great power, when, in fact, Jesus stripped him of it.

James, the brother of Jesus, gets right to the point in his letter to the church...*Resist the devil [stand firm against him], and he will flee from you.* The "understood" subject of this sentence is **you**...*You* resist the devil. Jesus defeated him at the cross and stripped him of his authority, but it's still up to us to *resist* him. That's why praying for God to get the devil off our back is unscriptural. That's our job.

In his painting, *Tying the Knots in the Devil's Tail,* western artist George Phippen captured the epitome of **resisting,** which truly is an *active,* not *passive,* verb. These two cowpokes, rather than succumb to the devil's temptation, decide to have a little heading and heeling practice. I like to think of the header's rope being the *Word of God,* while the heeler's lariat is the *name of Jesus.* These two tools are available to every believer in resisting any temptation, accusation, or deception that Satan tries on us. Remember, he is a defeated foe.

Sam Ed Spence

Colossians 2:15 AMP *1 Corinthians 15:45*
Isaiah 53:12   *James 4:7 AMP*

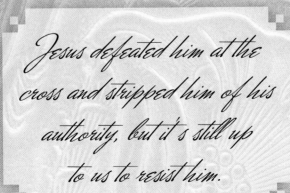

Jesus defeated him at the cross and stripped him of his authority, but it's still up to us to resist him.

Getting in Step

What we've learned is this: God does not respond to what we do: we respond to what God does. We've finally figured it out. Our lives get in step with God and all others by letting him set the pace, not by proudly or anxiously trying to run the parade.

Romans 3:27-28 The Message

Someone once said that one of the greatest revelations a man receives is when he discovers that he is not God.

That revelation entails an understanding that you cannot save yourself...regardless of doing mighty and wonderful things...regardless of keeping and never breaking the Ten Commandments...*For by grace are you saved by faith; and that not of yourselves: it is a gift of God: Not of works, lest any man should boast.*

After that salvation experience—being born again —there begins the process of getting in step with God in the various areas of our lives. The Apostle Paul put it this way in Romans...*be not conformed to this world: but be transformed by the renewing of your mind, that you may prove what is that good, and acceptable, and perfect will of God.*

It's a lot like breaking and training a horse—once

you've got the buck out of him, you have to bring him around to your way of thinking in each step he takes. It's a process, because he's been so used to doing everything *his way.* So have we.

We have to come around to God's way of thinking. We do that by renewing our mind with His Word. And what a wonderful thing to discover that God's way is so superior, so rewarding, so peaceful...so much better than when we were running the show!

God told the prophet Jeremiah, *"For I know the thoughts and plans that I have for you, says the Lord, thoughts and plans for welfare and peace and not for evil, to give you hope in your final outcome."*

How's that for incentive to turn the reins over to Him... let Him set the pace...getting in step with the Master!
Sam Ed Spence

   Ephesians 2:8-9   *Romans 12:2*
   1 John 2:15-16   *Jeremiah 29:11 AMP*

...God's way is so superior, so rewarding, so peaceful...so much better than when we were running the show!

Getting the Kinks Out
Tom Chapman

In the Hot Box with Jesus

...let us lay aside every weight, and the sin that so easily ensnares us, and let us run with endurance the race that is set before us. Hebrews 12:1

One would almost think that the Holy Spirit had jockeys in mind when He dictated this scripture to the writer of Hebrews. Those few extra pounds, that unwanted weight which so easily attaches itself to the body is something that a majority of race riders must deal with. And most of them, at one time or another, go to the hot box or whirlpool to sweat off the excess pounds in an effort to "make weight."

Of course, the weight the Bible refers to is anything in our life that would hinder the plans and destiny that God has for us...not *just* the plan for us eventually making it into heaven, but realizing and experiencing the victories and fulfillment in the midst of the race. In other words, God intends us to enjoy the journey (race). Jesus said, *"I've come that they* (every believer, His sheep) *might have life, and that they may have it more abundantly."*

Yes, He did say there would be persecutions for the Word's sake and that we would have some tribulations in the world (obstacles on life's track), *"but be of good cheer, I have overcome the world."* Jesus lived a sinless life, then went to that cross to not only become our sin and pay the price for it, but to make provision for every need we would ever have. That's the *abundance* He was talking about. He has already totally provided for our every need in this life!

Some Bible scholars feel that the *"sin that so easily ensnares us"* in our topic scripture above is simply **doubt and unbelief.** The Apostle Paul tells us in Romans that *whatever is not from faith is sin.* And since doubt and unbelief are the opposite of faith, it's obvious that this is the sin that so easily keeps us from receiving the promises of God and the many tremendous benefits that were provided for us via the death, burial, and resurrection of our Lord Jesus Christ.

We all need to jump in the "hot box" with Jesus and shuck off these weights of doubt and unbelief that keep us from running the race of life the way He intended. We do that by immersing ourselves in His Word...*faith comes by hearing and hearing by the word of God.*

Through the person of the Holy Spirit, God will bring the Bible alive to you, making the Word a part of your very being. As that happens, pounds of doubt and unbelief will begin rolling off. Instead of sapping you of your strength, Jesus' hot box builds you up, refreshes your soul, and empowers you to *go the distance.* Making weight with Jesus is a blast! *Sam Ed Spence*

John 10:10   Romans 14:23

John 16:33   Romans 10:17

He has already totally provided for every need in this life!

Up Close and Personal

"And I will pray the Father, and He will give you another Helper, that He may abide with you forever -- the Spirit of truth, whom the world cannot receive, because it neither sees Him nor knows Him; but you know Him, for He dwells with you and will be in you.

John 14:17

It just doesn't get any more *up close and personal* than Jesus living on the inside of you. But that's exactly what happened the moment you were born again. He came—in the person of the Holy Spirit—and made His abode (home) in you. Suddenly, you became the temple of the living God, the holy of holies...the same Spirit that raised Christ Jesus from the dead dwells in you!

It's down right mind boggling; in fact, the "religious" mind simply can't accept it...the very idea that the Creator of the universe lives—makes His home—inside of you. That means that wherever you go, God goes... remember His promise, *"I'll never leave you nor forsake you"*... you simply can't get away from Him; regardless of where you go or what you do, He's still right there on the inside of you.

"But what if I sin?"

He's still there; hasn't moved one iota...still available,

still forgiving, still loving, still in His same dwelling place.

"But I thought sin separates you from God!"

Only in your *mind.* The Holy Spirit never moves just because you "miss the mark." He just keeps on keeping on, right in His snug little abode of your heart. Regardless of those *unworthy* thoughts your mind comes up with, regardless of the *condemnation* the devil throws at you, God never pulls up stakes and vacates you.

In fact, the Holy Spirit is your number one fan and cheerleader. The Greek word for Holy Spirit is translated in the *Amplified Bible* as Comforter, Counselor, Helper, Intercessor, Advocate, Strengthener and Standby—a proverbial One-Man army with the power and wisdom of the universe living inside you.

That's about as *up close and personal* as it gets! *Sam Ed Spence*

Romans 8:11	*Romans 8:1*
Hebrews 13:5	*Colossians 1:21*
John 14:26	

...regardless of the condemnation
the devil throws at you,
God never pulls up stakes and
vacates you.

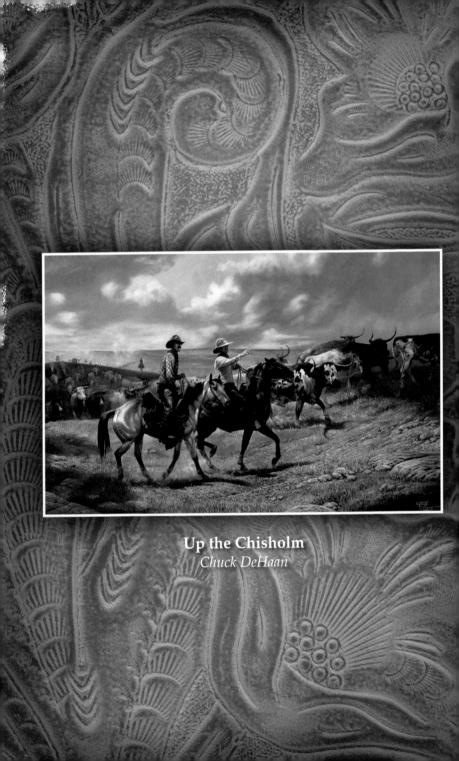

Up the Chisholm
Chuck DeHaan

The Great Roundup

"But when the Son of Man comes in his glory, and all the angels with him, then he will sit upon his glorious throne. All the nations will be gathered in his presence, and he will separate them as a shepherd separates the sheep from the goats. He will place the sheep at his right hand and the goats at his left."

Matthew 25:31-33 NLT

An old cowboy song goes "They say there will be a great roundup, where cowboys like doggies will stand, to be marked by the riders of judgment, who are posted and know every brand."

In the day of the big ranches and open range, during the roundups in certain geographical areas, a representative of each large ranch would attend the gatherings—actually, help gather. He would cut out the cattle from his ranch according to the brands and markings, then move them back to the home range.

The Bible tells us that on a certain day in the future, mankind will be sorted into two groups, according to the brand they have accepted in this life. The Bible says that God looks on the heart, not on the outside as man does. On our heart, we pack the brand of the cross of Jesus Christ, if we have given our heart to Him. Those who have been on the devil's range pack his brand...

the devil has more than a bad summer range planned for them.

In the old days, when the herd to be moved was large, they would sometimes brand the cattle with a road brand that changed the original. When we move to the Lord's range, we are branded again...with His brand. Make sure that's the brand you carry. Remember, God loves you. *Pete Crisswell*

Daniel 7:13   *Luke 12:32*
Revelation 20:11, 12   *1 Samuel 16:7*

The Bible says that God looks on the heart, not on the outside as man does.

About the Writers

Sam Ed Spence, 66, has been the "padre" at Lone Star Park in Grand Prairie, TX, since the track opened in 1997. Prior to that, he served two years as chaplain at Trinity Meadows Race Course in Willow Park, TX. A graduate of Texas A&M University, Sam has served as assistant editor of *The Quarter Horse Journal,* founding editor of *The Paint Horse Journal,* executive secretary of the American Paint Horse Assn., executive director of Quarter Racing Owners of America, Race Track Chaplaincy of America and Race Track Chaplaincy of Texas. He also pastored a non-denominational church near Keller, TX for ten years. He and his wife of 38 years, Margie, make their home in Southlake, TX.

Ed Donnally, 62, has been the Director of Development for Race Track Chaplaincy of America since 2001. A jockey on leading Thoroughbred tracks for 19 years, Ed studied English and journalism at the University of Delaware, University of Maryland and Eckard College in Florida. The former turf editor for *The Dallas Morning News,* he won the Eclipse Award for newspaper writing in 1984. Ed majored in Bible at Berean University in Los Angeles, and in 2001 was licensed as a minister in the Foursquare Church. He and his wife, Sandi, live in San Gabriel, CA.

Pete Crisswell, 60, has been a race track chaplain since 1983, when he pioneered the chaplaincy program at Delta Downs, Vinton, LA. A former jockey who hung up his irons in 1979, Pete has served as the chaplain at Louisiana Downs in Bossier City, Fair Grounds in New Orleans, Remington Park in Oklahoma City, and the New Mexico tracks in Albuquerque, El Paso (Sunland Park), and Farmington, as well as fair circuit tracks in California. He is currently the chaplain at the newly rebuilt track, Evangeline Downs, Opelousas, LA.